Meeting Mogwyn

A Glimpse into the Victorian Past

Colin Edward Mason

Copyright © Colin Edward Mason

All rights reserved.

ISBN: **149596258X**
ISBN-13: **978-1495962585**

DEDICATION

To Nanny Fitch

Celia Sanger

CONTENTS

   Acknowledgments i

1 Introduction 1

2 Meeting Mogwyn 13

3 About the Author 43

ACKNOWLEDGMENTS

Thank you to volunteer editors Jenny Clarkson, Valerie Ann Hamilton, Maureen (Mogwyn) Sutton for reading through and giving extremely valuable feedback. A big thank you also to Nicola Streeten and the Beacon Art Project for organizing a most enjoyable trip to the Profusion Exhibition at Calke Abbey in Summer 2010. Lastly, thank you to author Lisa Marie Gabriel for a final proofread and introduction, advice and help with the technical issues of publishing.

1 INTRODUCTION

You are about to read what I believe is a true ghost story, although Colin Mason reserves judgment on that and does not want to play up the supernatural or spooky aspects of his experience. In his own words:

"The following story is true. A chance meeting with an old friend led on to an unexpected coach trip to an old, reputedly, haunted abbey. Neither the author nor his friend had previously heard of Calke Abbey and neither anticipated anything other than a pleasant day among the Derbyshire peaks and, maybe, a glimpse into the Victorian past.

It was whilst gazing out of the window of an upstairs room cluttered with Victorian bric-a-brac that the author had a strange, perhaps ghostly experience! Did the unexpected coach trip lead on to an experience of the supernatural? Was it a Time Anomaly? Was it no more than the babble of an overactive imagination creating a striking coincidence? Always supposing, that is, that you believe in coincidence!"

Bearing that in mind, Meeting Mogwen is not just a "true ghost story". It is an essay that details the experience of the whole day, a response to the Profusion Exhibition and a memoir of his visit to Calke Abbey, which is in fact a stately home known internationally as the house that time forgot!

In meeting Mogwyn, the author writes of the circumstances of his trip to Calke Abbey, describing how the trip came about, his companions, thoughts, feelings and experiences of the whole day with close intimacy and fine detail. What some may consider a supernatural event is experienced in the context of this beautiful stately home, its attractions and the vivid presentation of a house preserved in its entirety with rare integrity.

Colin Mason was not aware before his visit of any hauntings although subsequently he found out that he was not the only visitor to Calke Abbey to experience the inexplicable. It is not necessary to believe in ghosts to enjoy the memoir of his day. Interestingly, the tale shows that even sceptics can experience a haunting.

Whether you believe in the existence of ghosts; or perhaps that all time co-exists making it possible to experience past events as though in a hologram; or that perhaps the stones of a building may "record" past events like a natural video recorder, Nanny Fitch was a real character and her presence, and that of others, was experienced many years after her death.

- *Lisa Marie Gabriel*

MEETING MOGWYN

Colin Edward Mason

2 MEETING MOGWYN

Over the past few months, it has become my custom to catch a bus at the bus stop about a hundred yards or so from the bungalow at Bracebridge Heath where I live. The bungalow is surrounded by a high Leylandii hedge which also encloses a garden that is becoming increasingly respectful of nature's primeval exuberance.

From Bracebridge Heath, I ride to Waddington, a distance of about a mile and a half, walk through the village, which I first visited about forty years ago, and then walk back along the ridge. Sometimes, I reverse the procedure; just for a change. Or, on those special mornings, when a seductive, warm breeze is sweeping friendly clouds across a benign, wide blue sky, I may be seduced into walking the entire circuit.

On this particular morning, I had decided to ride to and walk from Waddington. The bus, a number One to Grantham, would leave Lincoln bus station at eight thirty five to arrive at my chosen bus stop at ten to nine. I got there in good time.

It was a pleasantly warm morning with some clouds moving across the sky but they did not seem to interfere much with the steady sunlight. I glanced down at the small, square plastic travelling clock that I carry with me, bought in Boston, Lincolnshire three or four years ago under a year's guarantee, but still going and keeping good time.

The bus was due in a couple of minutes and soon I would see it coming towards me along the road winding between the bungalows with their tidy, reassuring lawns with neatly trimmed shrubs and bushes. The austere influence of Zen is clearly visible in the flowerless and calculatedly boulder studded precincts of 'DUNROAMIN'.

From the small and ugly heavy, brown-framed window of a bungalow opposite, a small dog was watching me. I stared back at him. I always stare back at babies too. At this point, I see the situation as if it were a film being shown on the T.V. between my ears as a Brooklyn voice in my head says,

"Dat kid's starin' at me! O. K. Buster, dat's fine wid me! Dat's how ya wannit, dat's how ya gonna git it! An' I stare right back at 'im!"

His mouth open, with his tongue hanging out, the dog sat still like an ornament. Then he glanced down to his left.

"Dat showed you, buddy-boy!"

Hope I didn't say the last bit out loud! He became momentarily agitated, glanced at me then back at whatever had become so much more important than this interspecies battle of wills.

I glanced at my clock. The bus was late. Perhaps the times change on Saturdays? The glass protecting the time-table had some kind of foggy white smear obscuring the departure times but from what I could make out, they were set unaltered from Monday to Saturday. The bus was late or else had made good time from the bus station and I had missed it. I decided to walk along the ridge to Waddington and ride back.

There are two footpaths along the top of the heath. They run, more or less parallel, either side a low barbed-wire fence over grown in places with dog-rose bushes and the remains of a quick-set hedge. The path on the village side of the fence marks the edge of a corn field whilst that on the other side follows a less defined course along the top of the heath.

As usual, I chose the heath path. It would eventually rejoin the field path which leads directly into a wooded dell where a sign in large, neat red letters on a white ground set low among the nettles under the spread of a densely leaved silver birch warns walkers, DEEP WATER KEEP OUT. A high, battered and bent, square mesh wire fence with two courses of barbed wire running parallel above it shields a large pond surrounded by trees.

The pond looks like a flooded, abandoned earth works of some sort. The path rises out of the dell to a swing-gate by which there stands another KEEP OUT sign, the words roughly painted in yellowing white paint on to a rusty metal panel attached to a rusty iron pole. The gate opens into a potato field with, because of a recent dry spell, sprinklers flashing unofficial rainbows in the fine spray pumped up from the dangerous deeps in the dell.

The path follows a high hedge around the heath side of the field but the hedge, though profuse and rich with a variety of wild undergrowth, comes to an abrupt end. There are now gnarled and crooked blackthorn trees with rough, grassy and bare earth spaces and fallen, rotting blackthorn trunks with broken branches, between them. Even on a sunny day there is a brooding ambiance of lonely moorland pervading this spot. This would be a suitable setting, perhaps, for the fateful game of chess with the Grim Reaper.

Almost as abruptly as it stopped, the hedge resumes its course and leads to another, overgrown, narrow path that descends through a virtual tunnel of dog roses, quick-set and elder, then up and along more or less level to the end of Far Lane, Waddington. All along, this, the Viking Way, the view from the high heath path is a broad, flat patchwork of fields that stretch to a blue-gray horizon of hills on the other side of the wide valley with the white-plumed cooling towers of three power stations in a distant row, rising out of clumps of trees.

This valley, I have been told, was scooped out of the earth and rock by gigantic ice-flows God (and maybe some geologist somewhere sipping cocoa in a frozen tin hut) knows how many thousands of years ago. Even still, rocks some of them the size of gravestones, lie where they were dumped when the ice grew tired and melted.

In Waddington, I made for Bar Lane which leads to the main road, a supermarket and a bus stop. On the way I would pass the `Horse and Jockey', a traditional village inn, sadly `improved' in places inside but the exterior facing the High street, has changed little since I first knew it and has retained its picture-postcard village pub appearance.

The Horse and Jockey is also a stopping place for buses. Not for the number One that I intended to use but the right one for Mogwyn! Each surprised to see the other; this was one of few and far between chance meetings.

I am always pleased to meet Mogwyn. I had first met her in the nineteen sixties when she was much involved with folk music at the Turk's Head, a Lincoln pub with an Elizabethan style exterior, near Newport Arch, built, I think, in the nineteen twenties. She sang with a fine, strong mezzo contralto voice and had an easy going, friendly manner with an underlying firmness most markedly expressed in her egalitarian view of life.

Her studies in local history seem to have uncovered in her a deep rooted empathy with people in whom ambition, if incompatible with their God ordained station, would have been considered sedition.

Though never overbearingly political in conversation, it soon becomes clear that Mogwyn hates injustice. She is a published writer, `We Didn't Know Aught,' and `A Lincolnshire Calendar,' were published by Paul Watkins. She has an extensive knowledge of Lincolnshire customs, and is a regular contributor to Lincolnshire Life Magazine. Also, she is in demand as a popular and authoritative speaker. She gives the impression of very down to earth practicality, occasionally laced with bawdiness which I have, for some time thought to be a personal defence mechanism. Her sensitivity tends to leak out rather than be overtly displayed. Being about five feet two inches tall, Mogwyn also affords me the rare distinction of glancing upwards to meet my gaze!

Conscious that we would not have long to chat, we did our best at small talk. I rhapsodised about the splendours of the high heath ridge, the trees, the view and the sheer joy of being there. Mogwyn commented on` the stunning view' and we agreed that we were both fortunate to be where we were. Then I remembered that as Lisa and I had only recently moved from town to Bracebridge Heath, Mogwyn would not have our new address and phone number. I quickly put that right.

Not having the pencil and note book that I usually carry with me in a small cloth pouch attached to a long loop of cord draped around my neck and under my fleece so that it hangs at about hip level, Mogwyn wrote the information on an old bus ticket. She glanced at her watch as I asked about the buses that stopped at the `Horse and Jockey'. Her expression changed from one of smiling, gray-blue eyed pleasantness to one of slightly harassed concern. The bus would appear in a few seconds time.

"Oh, Colin," she said. "There's a coach trip to Calke Abbey in Derbyshire! It's only five quid, and that includes entry to the abbey!"

I had never heard of Calke Abbey but the thought of a coach trip to the Peaks seemed like almost supernatural good luck to me.

"The coach leaves from the museum at ten fifteen. It's short notice but if you can make it, it will be really worth it! A trip like that for five quid!"

I agreed and said that I would get back to Bracebridge Heath as quickly as I could and see how it fitted in with the `memsaab's' plans for the day. The bus came into view and slowed down as it approached the old inn. Mogwyn's expression became even more serious as the bus pulled up. Her lips were tightly pressed together and the corners of her mouth very sharp, almost as if she were vexed. Her eyes frowned as she reached into her shoulder- bag searching for her bus pass. It was almost as if she had put on a mask, so different, so un-Mogwyn-like was the face that I was looking at at that moment.

Still looking harassed but re-Mogwynated she said she would give me a call. I told her she would get the answering machine but that that did not mean we were not at home. She climbed onto the bus and it pulled away. I felt foolish for babbling on about the answering machine whilst Mogwyn was intent on boarding the bus and excavating her bus pass from the depths of her bag. I had decided that so long as it did not foul-up any essential business for the day, I would go to Derbyshire and Co? Coo? Cote? Caurt? Abbey.

I quickened my step to Bar Lane and thence to the main road and the bus stop where I was pleased to see a small, middle-aged- to- elderly lady waiting. I gave her a weak smile as I asked her which side of the bus stop marked the front of the queue? Her expression remained stern as she said it did not matter. I hoisted myself up to sit on the supermarket's low, slab capped boundary wall. My mind was full of images of Coot? Abbey. I saw, in my mind's eye, a medieval ruin with high, Gothic arches, weathered gargoyles and, maybe, stone likenesses of long dead stone carvers and others of contemporary significance inviting satire, admiration, or affectionate, albeit now anonymous, acknowledgement of a friend who lived when the stone was being carved.

The number One from Grantham to Lincoln via Bracebridge Heath pulled up. The lady boarded first and I soon after. I showed the driver my bus pass. Middle aged and heavy, he responded with a minimal glance. His face retained the blank expression of a mechanism switched off and forgotten about and hung on the front of his head because it had to be put somewhere. He tapped some buttons on the ticket machine and the ticket popped out. I took it, thanked the driver and went upstairs.

With my head full of plainsong and snippets from FRANCIS of ASSISI, A Portrait, E.M. Almedingen, I got off the bus at Bracebridge Heath and covered the hundred yards or so from the bus shelter to our bungalow in less time than it takes to recite the Lord's Prayer backwards. Lisa was up and, as usual, at her computer.

"I've just met Mogwyn in Waddington!" I exclaimed. "And she says there's a coach trip to Derbyshire for only five pounds! It's going to something Abbey and the five pounds includes admission! Do we want to go?"

"That's good value for the trip alone," she replied. "But I can't afford to take the day off, I've got too much school work to do. You go. I know how much you like that sort of thing." There were one or two bits and pieces to be done, shopping, the lottery, feeding the fat feral at the old house in town but Lisa said she could see to them.

The coach would leave from the museum. Which museum? The museum of Lincolnshire Life or the City Museum, irritatingly called, 'The Collection'. The name, `The Collection` has, for me, the ring of early nineteen sixties affectation.

Mogwyn had not specified which museum. It had not occurred to her that the museum could mean anything other than The City Museum. It had not occurred to me either. We both like the building and its contents but for much the same reasons, dislike the name, `The Collection`.

Lisa thought it might be best to wait for another occasion as I might be wasting my time were I to rush into town only to find I had to gallop over a mile up the Steep, through the old city and along Burton Road to the Museum of Lincolnshire Life. The Lincoln bus would leave the nearby bus stop at about nine thirty seven. It would take, barring delays, about fifteen minutes to reach the bus station. The distance from the bus station to the museum is about half a mile. I decided I would try. With a ten pound note in my pocket I said bye-bye to Lisa.

"See you sooner or later, Frond!" Soon I was sitting on the bench in the sun shine by the bus shelter waiting for the number One.

It was a relief to see Mogwyn standing by the entrance to the City Museum. She smiled and was clearly pleased when she said,

"You made it!" I do not flatter myself that it was my personal presence that so pleased her but rather that she wanted to get 'bums on coach-seats' and that this bum would do as well as any.

"Only just!" I replied, "I was not sure, afterwards, which museum you meant! This one or the museum of Lincolnshire Life!"

"Oh, I'm sorry! I never thought of that! Have you been up there?"

"No, I came straight here and here you are."

"Yes, but I don't know where everybody else is. There's you, me and Jenny. I don't know where the rest are."

I did my best to help with rounding up fellow travelers. I asked a group of ladies sitting at a table in the museum cafe, were they waiting to board a coach to Derbyshire? They smiled and said they were not but one of them said that it was a nice idea. Several bemused strangers later, it was time to find a seat on the coach. That was not difficult. The coach was designed to carry fifty or sixty passengers. There were at first count, fifteen of us but a second count reduced the number to twelve.

The driver, a small good-natured man who spoke with a pleasing, Suffolk accent, said that at least we had plenty of space. He then, imitating an airline stewardess, mimed the safety procedures as the same drill was displayed on a screen just above his head. His cheerful nature communicated itself very easily and we were all, seven ladies and one other man, all of us from middle aged to elderly, quite happy to have the whole coach to ourselves. Mogwyn was the only one I knew although I had first met Jenny some years before at the Sun Cafe in Lincoln.

Upon my first acquaintance with Jenny, I had formed a negative impression of her. She seemed remote and to convey an impression of superiority which I had previously encountered among some of the members of poetry groups in other towns in other parts of the country. I had gained the impression, too, that the negative perception was mutual. I had met her again some months before in the company of Mogwyn. The negative ambiance was still there.

Be this so or no, I had decided that as it seemed likely that Mogwyn, Jenny and I were going form a group for the duration of this adventure, my supposed perception of this negativity was not going to be allowed to colour my overt attitude towards Jenny. The three of us sat in separate seats on the coach, I behind Mogwyn, Jenny behind me, all three of us not far from the front.

We could each sit by a window! There would be no obligation to make attempts at conversation to pass the time or just be sociable. This arrangement was Jenny's idea. The negative perception, so far as I was concerned, was beginning to soften!

The coach grunted, then growled and we were on our way. This was perfect and totally unexpected. Had the Waddington bus been on time, I would not have met Mogwyn outside the Horse and Jockey. I would have known nothing of the trip and would not now be sitting on a coach heading for Coo what's its name Abbey. Visions of peaks and trees and stone built cottages virtually unchanged for centuries came to mind as we left Lincoln. Mogwyn had told me as we boarded the coach, that the organisers of the trip wanted us to produce a creative response to the event.

I had at first been dismissive of the idea. It seemed too much like, art on demand. At this point, I still had no idea what my creative response might be and even less idea as to whom `they' were. Also, at this point I had no reason to expect the strange, possibly supernatural event I was destined to experience: an event that has made me question still further the true nature of time beyond our sequential experience of it!

My present concern as I gazed contentedly out of the window, was the landscape. I savoured the brief glimpses into other peoples' lives in back to backs with cluttered gardens; in bungalows with tidy lawns or cars pulled to pieces in not so tidy back yards; the sense of life being experienced in this scramble of cluttered, passing images; playing fields with 'someone running up to bowl,' J.C.Bs gouging out chunks of hedgerow and green field. All of this made me long for the days of 'Merry England' but with the National Health, high tech medical provision and universal manhood suffrage.

Not too bothered about the telly, though, there's rarely anything worth bothering with, except for the news, history programs, and Pride and Prejudice with Jenifer Ehle and Colin Firth (but scrap the unconvincing swimming scene, Ms Austin made a much better, more credible job of the unexpected encounter).

Soon, or so it seemed, Nottinghamshire horizons were dipping and rising into Derbyshire. As the coach hummed and then whined up a hill, we approached a power station, its hard-faced cooling towers rising high and intimidating from among densely leaved trees. Fascinating and vaguely, frightening, the huge towers aligned and realigned like the poisonous vapour-plumed columns of a huge temple as we passed by them.

There would be times, I thought, when the vapours would be dense, and, rising high, stand still in a breeze-less sky looking solid as if cast in concrete. They would combine with heavy clouds to produce an apocalyptic sense of enormous mass and threatening weight.

The child within me that was afraid of the dark and expected the end of the world with every fiery sunset would wonder how all that towering tonnage could stay suspended!

A steeple-less church on a distant, sheer rock-faced hill brought to mind the Abbey that couldn't be so far off now. Was it part of it? Would we approach it through winding lanes rising, twisting and descending through rich, green tunnels of leaves and branches full of birds and all the sounds and flickering green leaved lights of glorious sun-shiny, shimmering heat-hazy summer?

No. Soon after we left the main road, the driver was as lost as I was! For a while, we moved at the pace of the horse and cart that trundled along the lane in front of us. This couldn't have been better if it had been planned. The day was warm and sunny, the countryside was lovely and the whole company giggled and breathed a communal sigh of total bliss.

Eventually, after a couple of mobile phone calls and directions from an old man by the road side, Calke Abbey came into view. The sound of plainsong in my mind's ear came to an abrupt stop as the cerebral stylus skidded across my Gothic fantasy! In the cleft between the wooded hills that had been landscaped to form the deer park, there stood a solid Baroque country house with enough windows to impress even the fawning, sycophantic Mr Collins.

Before entering the house at three thirty, we had about ninety minutes to wander about in the grounds. We were greeted by a lady wearing an orange, short sleeved `T' shirt. This was Nicola, she was the organiser of the trip. After receiving our payments, she directed our attention to a man sitting at a table with several apples on it.

The man wore a black beret and a banded `T' shirt. (The truth is, I am not sure about the banded `T' shirt, but it would fit with the beret and the `Left Bank Blue Period,' image). His job was to look like an artist and to nibble the apples into portraits of people who sat and faced this or that direction as he instructed. Mogwyn was amused by the idea and decided to be apple-ated. While this was happening, Jenny got busy with pen and note paper working on her `creative response'.

I wandered about looking at buildings that probably had once been barns or storage spaces of some other sort to do with the maintenance of the house, grounds and country house life. Now they housed a public lavatory, a cafe and a shop that sold post cards and souvenirs. I bought some post cards as a substitute for wrapping up the day in a brown paper parcel and taking it home with me. I thought about buying a straw hat as a useful keepsake but decided that my white cotton, floppy sun hat would do.

I bought a small carton of pressed orange juice from a tiny refreshment shop housed in the end, sloping roofed section of a long brick built barn with stone capped steps at the other end leading up to an upper story, and then wandered back to see how Mogwyn was getting on.

She was still sitting and the sculptor was still nibbling, so Jenny and I watched for a while. When the nibbling was done, Mogwyn seemed pleased with the result but made a disparaging comment about her `conk', which is small quite pointed and turns down slightly at its tip. It would be vulgar flattery to describe her nose as being fine, but it is very definitely not the prodigious protuberance combining the characteristics of onion and bill hook that I suspect Mogwyn herself imagines it to be!

The three of us walked across the very warm and sunny park to the medieval but much altered church which we found to be fenced off so that we were unable to get in except by a special path somewhere out of our immediate reach. We wandered back towards the house past the ha-ha and chatted as we went about Mary Wollstonecraft and life in the eighteenth century.

My negative perception of Jenny had by now evaporated and feeling mildly embarrassed that I had ever harboured what seemed to be an inappropriate assessment of her personal character, I was reminded of the Buddhist teaching that we seldom perceive people as they really are but that we experience a projection of our own, usually self-interested, subjective response to them. Nicola had given us each a ticket which, along with location, date etc., had `ENTRY TIME 100' printed on it. The 100 had been scribbled out and 3.30 biroed in, then printed under it, `Other Free H&G'.

There was still about half an hour to go before we would be allowed into the house. Mogwyn had to collect her portrait. The sculptor kept the original and gave Mogwyn a photocopy of the sketch done from the apple. We agreed that sculpting a likeness from an apple, chiseling with incisors, was skillful but that the most lifelike quality of the original was its inevitable shriveling and decay. We sat at a table outside the refreshments shop, where Jenny took a photograph of Mogwyn and me, then, I took one of the ladies.

Looking at her portrait, Mogwyn said, "Seems a pity to fold it". As she curled the top edge of the paper over and began to make a crease at the middle of one edge, I said, "Don't fold it, wrap it around something and tie it with a piece of string".

She thought this a good idea and wrapped the paper around a mineral water bottle. We tied it in place with a strip of plastic torn from a small black plastic bag in which I carry two note books, one for Sanskrit studies, (which is hardly ever used) and one for attempts at poetry and sundry projects. Mogwyn was pleased.

Now it was time to go into the house. At the door, Nicola asked for our tickets, made a small rip in the top edge and handed them back to us. I was pleased to get my ticket back, because it would be a reminder of a day that was unfolding in a totally unexpected way.

When I, with probably childish glee, exclaimed, "Oh, we get to keep our tickets!" two or three other people in orange `T' shirts smiled and seemed pleased that I should want the souvenir.

My first impression on entering the old house was of high ceilings and stuffed birds and beasts. I have never understood the pleasure that some take in killing and then having their victims preserved. Although as a child I found it exciting to see the stuffed corpses of foxes, owls and eagles posed in threatening positions, albeit in glass cases, I had not yet come to think of them as having once been conscious, living beings with the capacity to experience their environment and being motivated by a powerful sense of the need to stay alive in it. The propaganda with which my childhood was flooded taught me that anything big with claws or teeth or both was by its very nature evil and should be killed - or at least caged. But I was now entering the Victorian world almost as if through a time portal.

I remember the disappointment close to anger that I had felt when I visited Shakespeare's house in the early nineteen sixties and saw that the interior had been plastered and painted white and the timbers painted black in order to conform to a misguided notion of what tourists would like to see. A small, glass-covered panel of the interior wattle that Shakespeare would have known and accepted as normal was all that remained of that once familiar part of his environment. No such falsifying sanitization had taken place here!

Room after room seemed to contain within it the imprint of the presence of its past occupants. I was overwhelmed by the sense of the every-day experience of those, now long dead, who had once lived there when I walked into a room with Gillray and Rowlandson satirical prints pasted on to the walls!

The prints themselves absorbed my attention. Common place and a joke to whomsoever it was that pasted them on to the walls, they were, to me, a precious thumb print of the indefinable, ungraspable present moment. I remember too, my embarrassment after I had left the room having, in my gushing enthusiasm, lectured the attendant on the significance of the 'wall paper'. She smiled kindly and assured me that she was aware of it. I prefer to believe that she took some pleasure in my unconcealed rapture.

Whenever I go into an old house or church containing old furniture, I feel impelled to touch the timber of which the things are made. I do this in the hope, rather than belief, that it may have retained some record of an event, however trivial, that may have occurred there. By touching the timber I might, by clearing my mind and making myself receptive, activate the dormant imprint like the laser beam scanning a C.D. and thereby establish some kind of sequential-time-barrier-banishing contact. This would enable me to eavesdrop on the event, conversation or individual utterance that the grain might have fixed within it.

Room after room seemed to contain within it the imprint of its former occupants! Up until the twenty sixth of June twenty ten, nothing extraordinary had ever happened. Nor am I sure that touching the woodwork had anything to do with the event that I am about to relate. As I look back now from the present time of writing, I cannot be sure that I was actually touching the wooden shutter as I gazed down through the upstairs window of a cluttered, Victorian room, across the park and on to the lake, trees and hills in the distance.

There was a sense of time enclosed in the space where I was standing. I heard, indistinctly at first, a man's voice. He was talking but I could not distinguish actual words.

Then, as clearly and distinctly as if the speaker were in the same room, I heard,

"Mrs Fitch!"

The voice was sharp and had a rising cadence that expressed some urgency. I was intrigued but thought it most likely to be just an invention of my occasionally noisy imagination. I have, in the past, in that no-man's-land between waking and sleeping, heard someone call my name even though, in reality, no one had. I have even seen the image of a stranger looking at me as if we were face to face and the stranger would utter a meaningless phrase. But in this instance, I was not on the verge of falling asleep.

As I have said, the voice was very clear. That, in its self, did not surprise me too much, as it was still easily within the realms of imagination. But I did have to question, why Mrs Fitch? Where did that name come from? I then pondered should I mention it to the attendant? Does the name Mrs Fitch have any significance or would I just embarrass myself? He would probably think me barmy!

I also thought that if I did not mention it, I would, in due course, wish that I had and would reproach myself for being timid. I would never know if the name, Mrs Fitch, which meant nothing to me, was that of someone who had been in some way associated with the room or with someone who had lived in the house. So I approached the attendant, a tall, quite heavily built man with a good natured expression and informally tidy grey hair and told him what I had just heard. I modified the nature of the experience slightly when I told him that the name Mrs Fitch had `come to mind'.

I also asked about the significance, if any, of that name. He looked a little startled at first and then said

"Nanny Fitch!"

I suddenly felt frightened. A shudder and a curiously cold, tense sensation passed through me almost like an electric shock. Up to that point and for the duration of the voice experience, I had not felt anything resembling fear. I was intrigued but thought it most likely to be just an invention of my, perhaps, theatrical imagination. But here was independent confirmation!

I think my discomposure must have been apparent for he told me that the spirits had spoken to me, that there were a lot of spirits in the house but they could not harm us.

"Let me show you something," he said and he led me back to a room through which I had just passed.

He directed my attention to the photograph of a stern faced Victorian lady wearing a plain, dark dress with a white lacy front. Her grey hair was centre-parted and covered at the crown of her head by an elaborate, lace-trimmed indoor cap with, perhaps, a widow's peak.

It is possible that the stern expression was the result of her having to sit very still as the photographic plate was being exposed.

Displayed in an elaborately moulded but chipped gilded frame, it hung quite high up in the semi-darkness on the pale, vaguely pinkish orange floral papered wall. He said that we were probably in her room or that hers may have been the room where I heard her name so clearly and distinctly called.

The unease that had briefly troubled me had given way to a feeling of self-consciousness as I told him of my reluctance to talk about it at all since most people would think me barmy! He laughed and said that he did not think that at all because he was a member of the spiritualist church. So far as he was concerned, the spirits were as real as we two now talking about them.

He said that some people could communicate with the spirits and perhaps I was one of them. He told me about the kitchen which was said to be haunted and thought that maybe I should go down there and see if anything happened. He reassured me again and, laughing, said there was nothing barmy about my experience, "Unless we're both barmy!"

My personal prejudice gravitates against spirits theory. I favour the concept of a time anomaly. Put briefly, it is as if events exist in, or create, 'time spheres'. A time anomaly occurs when, for some unknown reason, the spheres overlap or merge into each other, the point of intersection creating a 'time bubble' that occupies space-time in both spheres thus causing the anomaly.

The testimony of some of the attendants affirms that a number of people have experienced unusual, not readily explicable, events in that part of the house.

So far as I know, there is no concrete, scientific evidence to support the time anomaly theory but I should emphasise that the `spirits' did not speak to me! I heard someone (Mrs. Fitch) being addressed! It is also possible that the name` Fitch' had entered my subconscious without my being aware of it from another source in no way related to the abbey and well before I went there.

Could it be that the` Upstairs Downstairs' scenario, still very much in evidence at Calke Abbey, had stimulated my imagination to produce a fragment of a potential scene in a T.V. drama? This is possible but it strains coincidence to a point that tests credibility so that the coincidence itself becomes remarkable.

It has also been suggested that the `stone tape' phenomenon could be the cause of these experiences. The `stone tape' theory postulates the idea that the stone of which a building is constructed records certain events that take place in it and that some people, sometimes referred to as `sensitives,' trigger the effects. My wood-touching custom, mentioned above, comes under the `stone tape' umbrella. It seems that people who have suffered physical trauma, especially electric shock or head injury, may be sensitised to the stone tape effect.

In nineteen seventy eight, I myself, suffered a subdural rupture, or cerebral haemorrhage, in a motorcycle accident. Have I been sensitized? Possibly, but not everyone reporting unusual experiences in that part of the house had suffered severe physical trauma!

Mogwyn and Jenny were beginning to feel tired and overloaded with stuff to absorb.

"There's too much to take in, in one go!" said Mogwyn as we made our way towards the servants' tunnel and the kitchen.

Whereas I enjoyed walking in the tunnel, Jenny found it disturbing. "I don't like this", she murmured.

In light of this, I thought it best not to prolong her discomfort so when we passed the entrance to the kitchen I decided not to urge a visit. I also quietly wished that the attendant had not told me that the kitchen was said to be haunted. Expectation creates a barrier and may encourage, albeit sincere, misinterpretation of natural phenomena. Self spooking!

Soon we were back in the open air where Nicola led us to a saw-pit with planks of wood piled into it in a way that suggested, to me, the random fall of match sticks spilled from a box by a careless, or maybe drunken, giant trying to light a fag. The planks had various statements written on them in different fonts.

The various fonts gave visual form to the verbal statements that resonated in a way almost equivalent to a tone of voice or accent. The piece explores, in this respect, the power of the written word to create a `sound' in the reader's consciousness.

This, as I write about the idea now, brings to mind the Hitler tortoise in` The Perishers,' with his shell shaped like a world war two German coalscuttle helmet and the words in his speech bubble written in black letter! From this, in tandem with syntactical clues, we know that the tortoise speaks with a German accent.

Our guide then turned to the original purpose of the pit, telling us that the terms `Top dog' and `Underdog,' had their origin in the saw pit where tree trunks were cut into planks with a long saw that had a cross-wise handle at both ends. The top-dog stood in the fresh air and pushed and pulled in coordination with the under-dog who pushed and pulled in the dark and dusty pit like an energetic and habitually industrious corps standing in a grave, working hard to keep body and soul apart.

During the coach trip back to Lincoln, for which we sat in separate seats as before, Jenny showed Mogwyn some of her recent poems. Mogwyn read them with interest and responded with pleasure. She seemed impressed. Jenny then passed the folder to me saying that I could read them, too, if I wanted to and that there was no need to comment.

The poems seemed to carry with them a strong, enclosed atmosphere. In one of them she had used words in a way that gave them an almost physical presence. I felt that I had, to some extent, experienced what it was like to be Jenny. When I told her this as I handed the folio back to her, she said,

"You've hit the nail on the head!"

She went on to explain her reason, for writing them. I am now inclined to think that it was Jenny who had hit the nail on the head.

On the way back to the museum, the driver stopped the coach to allow Jenny to get off near to the end of the street where she lived. As she left her seat, she said bye-bye to Mogwyn, and, turning to me, said

"Bye bye, it's been nice to have the chance to get to know you better".

The feeling was entirely mutual. The coach carried on to the museum where all except Mogwyn and I alighted.

The driver had overheard us discussing our means of returning from Lincoln to Bracebridge Heath and Waddington respectively. We thought we might go halves on a taxi but as his route back to Sleaford would take him through both villages, the driver said that he would give us a lift.

With just Mogwyn and I as passengers, the coach set off again from the museum, down the High Street, that at some point, metamorphoses into Newark Road, then turned off up Cross o' Cliff Hill. As the coach drew in to the curb at the bus stop near The Homestead at Bracebridge Heath, I thanked Mogwyn again for letting me know about the trip. She said she would be in touch with me with details of another trip to Calke Abbey to which I now look forward with eager anticipation.

The National trust, have in my opinion, adopted the right policy in preserving the abbey in, as near as possible, exactly the condition in which they acquired it. As I stepped down off the coach I thanked the driver, especially for the improvised tour of the leafy lanes near the noble pile. The doors shut behind me and as the coach drew away, I waved bye-bye to Mogwyn.

ABOUT THE AUTHOR

Colin Edward Mason was born in Kenilworth, Warwickshire in 1944, hated school and escaped, as soon as the law allowed, to the Mid-Warwickshire School of Art, Leamington Spa, and then to Hornsey College of Art London.

He worked in a variety of non-art related jobs, mostly labouring work, before becoming an Art and General Studies Teacher in a Secondary Modern School and later An Art and Art History Tutor in a Further Education College, both in Lincolnshire.

Colin Mason has exhibited work around Lincolnshire and in Yorkshire; with exhibitions in the theatre foyer in Hull with Severn Artists and at the Usher Gallery with electro mechanical sculptor Keith Carter. He won first prize in the Willoughby Art Competition, 1983 and first prize of £1000 in the 21st Century Life-stile Design A Quote Competition, a National Competition advertised in Artists' Newsletter in 1996. He has executed a number of professional illustration commissions but prefers to work independently on personal projects.

He is author and illustrator of The Cat the Bat and the Burglar, published by The Realm of Photahsiamirabel, and he is currently working on another book intended to present his more serious writing in something close to graphic novel format.

Colin Edward Mason

Printed in Great Britain
by Amazon